Animal Baby Bibs

Take your toddler on a pretend-trip to the zoo
with these fun bibs at breakfast, lunch, or dinner.

Meet Kristi Simpson

Inspired by her love of yarn, Kristi Simpson enjoys creating crochet and knit patterns with a fresh and modern touch.

The mother of five became hooked on crochet after teaching herself so she could help her daughter make a scarf from a "learn to crochet" kit that was a gift.

"I loved it from the beginning," she says. "I was amazed that I could take a string of yarn and create something so useful and pretty! Needless to say, I never stopped!"

Her designs have been published in several books and more than 50 magazine features. To see more of her designs, visit kristisimpson.net or find her on Ravelry, Facebook, and Pinterest.

LEISURE ARTS, INC. • Maumelle, Arkansas

M000221431

TIGER

 **EASY**

Finished Size: 7½" wide x 6½" long (19 cm x 16.5 cm) excluding Ears

SHOPPING LIST

Yarn (Medium Weight) 4
[1.75 ounces, 80 yards
(50 grams, 73 meters) per ball]:
☐ Orange - 55 yards (50.5 meters)
☐ Black - 30 yards (27.5 meters)
☐ White - 15 yards (13.5 meters)

Crochet Hook
☐ Size G (4 mm)
or size needed for gauge

Additional Supplies
☐ Yarn needle

GAUGE INFORMATION
11 sc and 12.5 rows = 3" (7.5 cm)
Gauge Swatch: 3" wide x 2⅞" high
(7.5 cm x 7.25 cm)
With Orange, ch 12.
Row 1: Sc in second ch from hook
and in each ch across: 11 sc.
Rows 2-12: Ch 1, turn; sc in each sc
across.
Finish off.

STITCH GUIDE

SINGLE CROCHET 2 TOGETHER
(abbreviated sc2tog)
Pull up a loop in each of next 2 sc, YO
and draw through all 3 loops on hook
(**counts as one sc**).

HEAD
With Orange and beginning at top of
Head, ch 19.

Row 1 (Wrong side)**:** 2 Sc in second ch
from hook, sc in each ch across to last
ch, 2 sc in last ch: 20 sc.

Note: Loop a short piece of yarn
around the **back** of any stitch on
Row 1 to mark **right** side.

Rows 2-4: Ch 1, turn; 2 sc in first sc, sc
in each sc across to last sc, 2 sc in last
sc: 26 sc.

Rows 5-22: Ch 1, turn; sc in each sc
across.

Rows 23-25: Ch 1, turn; beginning in
first sc, sc2tog, sc in each sc across to
last 2 sc, sc2tog: 20 sc.

Edging: Ch 1, turn; beginning in
first sc, sc2tog, sc in each sc across
to last 2 sc, sc2tog; sc evenly across
end of rows; working in free loops of
beginning ch *(Fig. 4, page 31)*, sc in ch
at base of first sc, place marker in last
sc made for Tie placement, sc in each
ch across to last ch, place marker in sc
just made for Tie placement, sc in last
ch; sc evenly across end of rows; join
with slip st to first sc, finish off.

Tie
With **right** side facing, join Black with
slip st in either marked sc on Edging,
remove marker; ch 52, hdc in back
ridge of second ch from hook *(Fig. 2,
page 31)* and each ch across; slip st in
next sc on Edging, finish off.

Repeat for second Tie in remaining
marked sc.

FEATURES
Ear (Make 2)
With Orange and beginning at tip,
ch 2.

Row 1 (Right side)**:** 2 Sc in second ch
from hook.

Note: Mark Row 1 as **right** side.

Row 2: Ch 1, turn; 2 sc in each sc across: 4 sc.

Row 3: Ch 1, turn; 2 sc in first sc, sc in next 2 sc, 2 sc in last sc: 6 sc.

Rows 4-6: Ch 1, turn; sc in each sc across.

Row 7: Ch 1, turn; beginning in first sc, sc2tog, sc in next 2 sc, sc2tog; finish off leaving a long end for sewing.

Muzzle

With White, ch 5.

Row 1: Sc in second ch from hook and in each ch across: 4 sc.

Row 2 (Right side)**:** Ch 1, turn; sc in each sc across.

Note: Mark Row 2 as **right** side.

Row 3: Ch 1, turn; 2 sc in first sc, sc in next sc, sc2tog.

Row 4: Ch 1, turn; beginning in first sc, sc2tog, sc in next sc, 2 sc in last sc.

Rows 5 and 6: Ch 1, turn; sc in each sc across.

Place a marker around last sc on Row 6 to indicate top edge.

Row 7: Ch 1, turn; beginning in first sc, sc2tog, sc in next sc, 2 sc in last sc.

Row 8: Ch 1, turn; 2 sc in first sc, sc in next sc, sc2tog.

Row 9: Ch 1, turn; sc in each sc across.

Edging: Ch 1, turn; sc in each sc across; sc in end of each row across; working in free loops of beginning ch, sc in ch at base of first sc and in each ch across; sc in end of each row across; join with slip st to first sc, finish off leaving a long end for sewing.

NOSE

With Black, ch 5.

Row 1 (Right side)**:** Sc in back ridge of second ch from hook and each ch across: 4 sc.

Note: Mark Row 1 as **right** side and top edge.

Row 2: Turn; slip st in first sc, sc2tog, slip st in last sc; finish off leaving a long end for sewing.

Centering **wrong** side of Nose to **right** side of Muzzle, sew Nose even with top edge; then add nose line and mouth using straight stitch and backstitch *(see Embroidery Stitches, page 31)*.

Eye (Make 2)
OUTER
With White, ch 2.

Rnd 1 (Right side)**:** 6 Sc in second ch from hook; join with slip st to first sc.

Note: Mark Rnd 1 as **right** side.

Rnd 2: Ch 1, 2 sc in same st as joining and in each sc around; join with slip st to first sc, finish off leaving a long end for sewing.

CENTER
With Black, ch 2.

Rnd 1 (Right side)**:** 6 Sc in second ch from hook; join with slip st to first sc, finish off leaving a long end for sewing.

Sew **wrong** side of Center to **right** side of Outer Eye.

Stripes

SMALL (Make 5)

With Black, ch 2.

Row 1 (Right side)**:** 2 Sc in second ch from hook.

Note: Mark Row 1 as **right** side.

Row 2: Ch 1, turn; sc in each sc across.

Row 3: Ch 1, turn; 2 sc in each sc across: 4 sc.

Finish off leaving a long end for sewing.

LARGE (Make 2)

Work same as Small Stripe through Row 3: 4 sc.

Row 4: Ch 1, turn; sc in each sc across.

Row 5: Ch 1, turn; 2 sc in first sc, sc in next 2 sc, 2 sc in last sc; finish off leaving a long end for sewing.

FINISHING

Using photo as a guide for placement and with **right** sides of all pieces facing:
Sew Ears to Head.

Sew 2 Small Stripes on each side of Head and the remaining Small Stripe at center top edge of Head. Sew Large Stripes at each side of center Small Stripe. Sew Muzzle and Eyes in place.

With Black, add straight stitch whiskers to Muzzle.

ZEBRA

 **EASY**

Finished Size: 7½" wide x 6½" long (19 cm x 16.5 cm) excluding Ears

SHOPPING LIST

Yarn (Medium Weight) 🧶 MEDIUM 4
[1.75 ounces, 80 yards
(50 grams, 73 meters) per ball]:
- ☐ Black - 40 yards (36.5 meters)
- ☐ White - 40 yards (36.5 meters)
- ☐ Green - 15 yards (13.5 meters)

Crochet Hook
- ☐ Size G (4 mm)
  or size needed for gauge

Additional Supplies
- ☐ Yarn needle

GAUGE INFORMATION

In Head pattern,
  11 sts and 8 rows = 3" (7.5 cm)
  11 sc and 12.5 rows = 3" (7.5 cm)
Gauge Swatch: 3" wide x 2⁷⁄₈" high
  (7.5 cm x 7.25 cm)
With Black, ch 12.
Row 1: Sc in second ch from hook
and in each ch across: 11 sc.
Rows 2-12: Ch 1, turn; sc in each sc
across.
Finish off.

STITCH GUIDE

SINGLE CROCHET 2 TOGETHER
  (abbreviated sc2tog)
Pull up a loop in each of next 2 sts, YO
and draw through all 3 loops on hook
(counts as one sc).

HEAD

With Black and beginning at top of
Head, ch 23; place marker in second
ch from hook for Trim placement.

Row 1 (Right side)**:** 2 Sc in second
ch from hook, sc in next 4 chs, hdc
in next 3 chs, dc in next 6 chs, hdc
in next 3 chs, sc in next 4 chs, 2 sc in
last ch: 24 sts.

Note: Loop a short piece of yarn
around any stitch to mark Row 1 as
right side.

Row 2: Ch 1, turn; 2 sc in first sc, sc in
next 5 sc, hdc in next 3 hdc, dc in next
6 dc, hdc in next 3 hdc, sc in next 5 sc,
2 sc in last sc changing to White in last
sc *(Fig. 3a, page 31)*; cut Black: 26 sts.

Row 3: Ch 2 **(does not count as a
st, now and throughout)**, turn; dc
in first 7 sc, hdc in next 3 hdc, sc in
next 6 dc, hdc in next 3 hdc, dc in
last 7 sc.

Row 4: Ch 2, turn; dc in first 7 dc,
hdc in next 3 hdc, sc in next 6 sc,
hdc in next 3 hdc, dc in last 7 dc
changing to Black in last dc *(Fig. 3b,
page 31)*; cut White.

Row 5: Ch 1, turn; sc in first 7 dc, hdc
in next 3 hdc, dc in next 6 sc, hdc in
next 3 hdc, sc in last 7 dc.

Row 6: Ch 1, turn; sc in first 7 sc, hdc
in next 3 hdc, dc in next 6 dc, hdc in
next 3 hdc, sc in last 7 sc changing
to White in last sc; cut Black.

Row 7: Ch 2, turn; dc in first 7 sc, hdc
in next 3 hdc, sc in next 6 sc, hdc in
next 3 hdc, dc in last 7 sc.

Rows 8-11: Repeat Rows 4-7.

Row 12: Ch 2, turn; dc in first 7 dc,
hdc in next 3 hdc, sc in next 6 sc, hdc
in next 3 hdc, dc in last 7 dc.

Rows 13 and 14: Ch 2, turn; dc in first st and in each st across.

Rows 15-18: Ch 1, turn; beginning in first st, sc2tog, sc in next st and in each st across to last 2 sts, sc2tog: 18 sc.

Finish off.

Trim: With **right** side facing, join White with sc in end of Row 18 *(see Joining With Sc, page 31)*; sc evenly across end of rows; working in free loops of beginning ch *(Fig. 4, page 31)*, sc in first 2 chs, place marker in last sc made for Tie placement, sc in each ch across to within one ch of next marker, remove marker and place marker in last sc made for Tie placement, sc in next 2 chs; sc evenly across end of rows ending in Row 18; finish off.

Tie

With **right** side facing, join Green with slip st in either marked sc on Trim, remove marker; ch 52, hdc in back ridge of second ch from hook *(Fig. 2, page 31)* and each ch across; slip st in next sc on Trim, finish off.

Repeat for second Tie in remaining marked sc.

7

Muzzle

Row 1: With **wrong** side facing and working in Back Loops Only *(Fig. 1, page 31)*, join Black with sc in first sc on Row 18; sc in next 17 sc: 18 sc.

Rows 2-6: Ch 1, turn; sc in both loops of each sc across.

Rows 7 and 8: Ch 1, turn; beginning in first sc, sc2tog, sc in each sc across to last 2 sc, sc2tog: 14 sc.

Finish off.

Trim: With **wrong** side facing, join Black with sc in end of Row 1; sc evenly across end of rows; sc in each sc across Row 8; sc evenly across end of rows; finish off leaving a long end for sewing.

Sew Muzzle to **right** side of Head.

FEATURES

Ear (Make 2)

With Black and beginning at tip, ch 2.

Row 1 (Right side): 2 Sc in second ch from hook.

Note: Mark Row 1 as **right** side.

Row 2: Ch 1, turn; 2 sc in each sc across: 4 sc.

Row 3: Ch 1, turn; 2 sc in first sc, sc in next 2 sc, 2 sc in last sc: 6 sc.

Rows 4-6: Ch 1, turn; sc in each sc across.

Row 7: Ch 1, turn; beginning in first sc, sc2tog, sc in next 2 sc, sc2tog; finish off leaving a long end for sewing.

Eye (Make 2)

OUTER

With White, ch 2.

Rnd 1 (Right side): 6 Sc in second ch from hook; join with slip st to first sc.

Note: Mark Rnd 1 as **right** side.

Rnd 2: Ch 1, 2 sc in same st as joining and in each sc around; join with slip st to first sc, finish off leaving a long end for sewing.

CENTER

With Black, ch 2.

Rnd 1 (Right side): 6 Sc in second ch from hook; join with slip st to first sc, finish off leaving a long end for sewing.

Sew **wrong** side of Center to **right** side of Outer Eye; then add eyelashes using straight stitches *(see Embroidery Stitches, page 31)*.

BOW

With Green, ch 9.

Row 1 (Wrong side): Sc in back ridge of second ch from hook and each ch across.

Note: Mark the **back** of Row 1 as **right** side.

Rows 2-4: Ch 1, turn; sc in each sc across; at end of Row 4, finish off.

Using Green, wrap the center of the Bow tightly approximately 10 times; tie knot on **wrong** side and leave a long end for sewing.

FINISHING

Using photo as a guide for placement, page 7, and with **right** side of all pieces facing:
Sew Ears to Head. Sew eyes in place. Sew Bow to Head near corner of Ear. Using a double strand of White, add straight stitch nostrils and a backstitch mouth.

COW

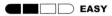 **EASY**

Finished Size: 7½" wide x 6½" long (19 cm x 16.5 cm) excluding Ears

Shown on page 11.

SHOPPING LIST

Yarn (Medium Weight)

[1.75 ounces, 80 yards
(50 grams, 73 meters) per ball]:

☐ White - 95 yards (87 meters)

☐ Pink - 22 yards (20 meters)

☐ Black - 12 yards (11 meters)

☐ Purple - small amount
(for optional Flower)

Crochet Hook

☐ Size G (4 mm)
or size needed for gauge

Additional Supplies

☐ Yarn needle

GAUGE INFORMATION

11 sc and 12.5 rows = 3" (7.5 cm)

Gauge Swatch: 3" wide x 2⁷/₈" high
(7.5 cm x 7.25 cm)

With White, ch 12.

Row 1: Sc in second ch from hook
and in each ch across: 11 sc.

Rows 2-12: Ch 1, turn; sc in each sc
across.

Finish off.

STITCH GUIDE

SINGLE CROCHET 2 TOGETHER
(abbreviated sc2tog)

Pull up a loop in each of next 2 sc, YO
and draw through all 3 loops on hook
(**counts as one sc**).

HEAD

With White and beginning at top of
Head, ch 19.

Row 1 (Wrong side)**:** 2 Sc in second ch
from hook, sc in each ch across to last
ch, 2 sc in last ch: 20 sc.

Note: Loop a short piece of yarn
around the **back** of any stitch on
Row 1 to mark **right** side.

Rows 2-4: Ch 1, turn; 2 sc in first sc, sc
in each sc across to last sc, 2 sc in last
sc: 26 sc.

Rows 5-22: Ch 1, turn; sc in each sc
across.

Rows 23-25: Ch 1, turn; beginning in
first sc, sc2tog, sc in each sc across to
last 2 sc, sc2tog: 20 sc.

Edging: Ch 1, turn; beginning in
first sc, sc2tog, sc in each sc across
to last 2 sc, sc2tog; sc evenly across
end of rows; working in free loops of
beginning ch *(Fig. 4, page 31)*, sc in
ch at base of first sc, place marker in
sc just made for Tie placement, sc in
each ch across to last ch, place marker
in last sc made for Tie placement, sc in
last ch; sc evenly across end of rows;
join with slip st to first sc, finish off.

Tie

With **right** side facing, join Pink with
slip st in either marked sc on Edging,
remove marker; ch 52, hdc in back
ridge of second ch from hook *(Fig. 2,
page 31)* and each ch across; slip st in
next sc on Edging, finish off.

Repeat for second Tie in remaining
marked sc.

FEATURES

Ear (Make 2)

With White and beginning at tip, ch 2.

Row 1 (Right side)**:** 2 Sc in second ch
from hook.

Note: Mark Row 1 as **right** side.

Row 2: Ch 1, turn; 2 sc in each sc across: 4 sc.

Row 3: Ch 1, turn; 2 sc in first sc, sc in next 2 sc, 2 sc in last sc: 6 sc.

Rows 4-6: Ch 1, turn; sc in each sc across.

Row 7: Ch 1, turn; beginning in first sc, sc2tog, sc in next 2 sc, sc2tog; finish off leaving a long end for sewing.

Muzzle
With Pink, ch 13.

Row 1 (Wrong side)**:** Working in back ridges of beginning ch, 2 sc in second ch from hook, sc in each ch across to last ch, 2 sc in last ch: 14 sc.

Note: Mark the **back** of Row 1 as **right** side.

Rows 2 and 3: Ch 1, turn; 2 sc in first sc, sc in each sc across to last sc, 2 sc in last sc: 18 sc.

Rows 4 and 5: Ch 1, turn; sc in each sc across.

Rows 6-8: Ch 1, turn; beginning in first sc, sc2tog, sc in each sc across to last 2 sc, sc2tog: 12 sc.

Finish off leaving a long end for sewing.

Spot
With Black, ch 2.

Rnd 1 (Right side)**:** 6 Sc in second ch from hook; do **not** join, place marker to indicate beginning of rnd *(see Markers, page 30)*.

Note: Mark Rnd 1 as **right** side.

Rnd 2: 2 Sc in each sc around: 12 sc.

Rnd 3: (Sc in next sc, 2 sc in next sc) around: 18 sc.

Rnd 4: (Sc in next 2 sc, 2 sc in next sc) around: 24 sc.

Rnd 5: (Sc in next 3 sc, 2 sc in next sc) around: 30 sc.

Rnd 6: (Sc in next 4 sc, 2 sc in next sc) around; slip st in next sc, finish off leaving a long end for sewing.

With a double strand of White, embroider a line around the edge of the Spot using running stitch *(see Embroidery Stitches, page 31)*.

Outer Eye
With White, ch 4.

Rnd 1 (Right side)**:** 8 Dc in fourth ch from hook; join with slip st to top of beginning ch-4, finish off leaving a long end for sewing.

Eye (Make 2)
With Black, ch 2.

Rnd 1 (Right side)**:** 4 Sc in second ch from hook; join with slip st to first sc, finish off leaving a long end for sewing.

Sew **wrong** side of one Eye to **right** side of Outer Eye.

FLOWER (Optional)
With Purple, ch 2.

Rnd 1 (Right side)**:** 7 Sc in second ch from hook; do **not** join, place marker to indicated beginning of rnd.

Note: Mark Rnd 1 as **right** side.

Rnd 2: (Slip st, ch 1, dc, ch 1, slip st) in each sc around; finish off leaving a long end for sewing.

FINISHING
Using photo as a guide for placement and with **right** side of all pieces facing:
Sew Ears to Head.
With a double strand of White, backstitch a mouth on Muzzle. With a double strand of Black, straight stitch an "X" for each nostril. Sew Muzzle to Head.
Sew Outer Eye to Spot; then sew Spot and remaining Eye to Head.
Optional: Sew Flower to Ear.

GIRAFFE

 **EASY**

Finished Size: 7½" wide x 6¾" long (19 cm x 17 cm) excluding Ears & Horns

SHOPPING LIST

Yarn (Medium Weight)

[1.75 ounces, 80 yards
(50 grams, 73 meters) per ball]:

- ☐ Yellow - 60 yards (55 meters)
- ☐ Tan - 35 yards (32 meters)
- ☐ Brown - small amount

Crochet Hook

- ☐ Size G (4 mm)
  or size needed for gauge

Additional Supplies

- ☐ Yarn needle

GAUGE INFORMATION

11 sc and 12.5 rows = 3" (7.5 cm)
Gauge Swatch: 3" wide x 2⁷/₈" high
  (7.5 cm x 7.25 cm)
With Yellow, ch 12.
Row 1: Sc in second ch from hook
and in each ch across: 11 sc.
Rows 2-12: Ch 1, turn; sc in each sc
across.
Finish off.

STITCH GUIDE

SINGLE CROCHET 2 TOGETHER
(abbreviated sc2tog)
Pull up a loop in each of next 2 sc, YO
and draw through all 3 loops on hook
(counts as one sc).

HEAD

With Yellow and beginning at top of
Head, ch 13; place marker in second
ch from hook for Trim placement.

Row 1 (Right side): 2 Sc in second ch
from hook, sc in each ch across to last
ch, 2 sc in last ch: 14 sc.

Note: Loop a short piece of yarn
around any stitch to mark Row 1 as
right side.

Rows 2-7: Ch 1, turn; 2 sc in first sc, sc
in each sc across to last sc, 2 sc in last
sc: 26 sc.

Rows 8-23: Ch 1, turn; sc in each sc
across.

Rows 24-26: Ch 1, turn; beginning in
first sc, sc2tog, sc in each sc across to
last 2 sc, sc2tog: 20 sc.

Edging: Ch 1, turn; beginning in
first sc, sc2tog, sc in each sc across
to last 2 sc, sc2tog; sc evenly across
end of rows; working in free loops of
beginning ch *(Fig. 4, page 31)*, sc in
first ch, place marker in sc just made
for Tie placement, sc in each ch
across to marked ch, remove marker
and place marker in last sc made
for Tie placement, sc in next ch; sc
evenly across end of rows; join with
slip st to first sc, finish off.

Tie

With **right** side facing, join Yellow
with slip st in either marked sc on
Edging, remove marker; ch 52, hdc in
back ridge of second ch from hook
(Fig. 2, page 31) and each ch across;
slip st in next sc on Edging, finish off.

Repeat for second Tie in remaining
marked sc.

FEATURES

Ear (Make 2)

With Yellow and beginning at tip, ch 2.

Row 1 (Right side): 2 Sc in second ch from hook.

Note: Mark Row 1 as **right** side.

Row 2: Ch 1, turn; 2 sc in each sc across: 4 sc.

Row 3: Ch 1, turn; 2 sc in first sc, sc in next 2 sc, 2 sc in last sc: 6 sc.

Rows 4-6: Ch 1, turn; sc in each sc across.

Row 7: Ch 1, turn; beginning in first sc, sc2tog, sc in next 2 sc, sc2tog; finish off leaving a long end for sewing.

Muzzle

With Tan, ch 19.

Row 1 (Wrong side): Working in back ridges of beginning ch, 2 sc in second ch from hook, sc in each ch across to last ch, 2 sc in last ch: 20 sc.

Note: Mark the **back** of Row 1 as **right** side.

Rows 2 and 3: Ch 1, turn; 2 sc in first sc, sc in each sc across to last sc, 2 sc in last sc: 24 sc.

Rows 4-8: Ch 1, turn; sc in each sc across.

Rows 9-12: Ch 1, turn; beginning in first sc, sc2tog, sc in each sc across to last 2 sc, sc2tog: 16 sc.

Finish off leaving a long end for sewing.

With a double strand of Brown, embroider a line around the edge of the Muzzle using running stitch *(see Embroidery Stitches, page 31)*.

Horn (Make 2)

With Tan, ch 2.

Rnd 1 (Right side): 6 Sc in second ch from hook; join with slip st to first sc.

Note: Mark Rnd 1 as **right** side.

Rnd 2: Ch 1, 2 sc in same st as joining and in each sc around; join with slip st to first sc: 12 sc.

Begin working in rows.

Row 1: Ch 1, turn; sc in first 2 sc, leave remaining 10 sc unworked.

Rows 2 and 3: Ch 1, turn; sc in first 2 sc.

Finish off leaving a long end for sewing.

Eye (Make 2)

With Brown, ch 2.

Rnd 1 (Right side): 6 Sc in second ch from hook; join with slip st to first sc, finish off leaving a long end for sewing.

FINISHING

Using photo as a guide for placement, page 13, and with **right** side of all pieces facing:
Sew Ears to Head Edging.
With a double strand of Brown, backstitch mouth on Muzzle. With a double strand of Brown, straight stitch an "X" for each nostril.
Sew Muzzle, Horns and Eyes to Head.

OWL

 EASY

Finished Size: 7½" wide x 6½" long (19 cm x 16.5 cm) excluding Wings

Shown on page 17.

SHOPPING LIST

Yarn (Medium Weight) 🔵4

[1.75 ounces, 80 yards
(50 grams, 73 meters) per ball]:

- ☐ Green - 45 yards (41 meters)
- ☐ Blue - 20 yards (18.5 meters)
- ☐ Tan - 19 yards (17.5 meters)
- ☐ Orange - 17 yards (15.5 meters)
- ☐ White - small amount
- ☐ Black - small amount

Crochet Hook

- ☐ Size G (4 mm)

  or size needed for gauge

Additional Supplies

- ☐ Yarn needle

GAUGE INFORMATION

11 sc and 12.5 rows = 3" (7.5 cm)

Gauge Swatch: 3" wide x 2⁷⁄₈" high
  (7.5 cm x 7.25 cm)

With Green, ch 12.

Row 1: Sc in second ch from hook
and in each ch across: 11 sc.

Rows 2-12: Ch 1, turn; sc in each sc
across.

Finish off.

STITCH GUIDE

TREBLE CROCHET *(abbreviated tr)*
YO twice, insert hook in st indicated,
YO and pull up a loop (4 loops on
hook), (YO and draw through 2 loops
on hook) 3 times.

SINGLE CROCHET 2 TOGETHER
  (abbreviated sc2tog)
Pull up a loop in each of next 2 sc, YO
and draw through all 3 loops on hook
(counts as one sc).

BODY

With Green and beginning at top of
Head, ch 21.

Row 1 (Wrong side)**:** 2 Sc in second ch
from hook, sc in each ch across to last
ch, 2 sc in last ch: 22 sc.

Note: Loop a short piece of yarn
around the **back** of any stitch on
Row 1 to mark **right** side.

Rows 2 and 3: Ch 1, turn; 2 sc in
first sc, sc in each sc across to last sc,
2 sc in last sc: 26 sc.

Rows 4-8: Ch 1, turn; sc in each sc
across.

Rows 9-11: Ch 1, turn; beginning in
first sc, sc2tog, sc in each sc across
to last 2 sc, sc2tog: 20 sc.

Row 12: Ch 1, turn; sc in each sc
across.

Row 13 (Increase row)**:** Ch 1, turn;
2 sc in first sc, sc in each sc across to
last sc, 2 sc in last sc: 22 sc.

Rows 14-17: Repeat Rows 12 and
13 twice: 26 sc.

Rows 18-23: Ch 1, turn; sc in each
sc across.

Rows 24 and 25: Ch 1, turn;
beginning in first sc, sc2tog, sc in
each sc across to last 2 sc, sc2tog:
22 sc.

Edging: Ch 1, turn; beginning in first sc, sc2tog, sc in each sc across to last 2 sc, sc2tog; sc evenly across end of rows; working in free loops of beginning ch *(Fig. 4, page 31)*, sc in ch at base of first sc, place marker in sc just made for Tie placement, sc in each ch across to last ch, place marker in last sc made for Tie placement, sc in last ch; sc evenly across end of rows; join with slip st to first sc, finish off.

Tie

With **right** side facing, join Orange with slip st in either marked sc on Edging, remove marker; ch 52, hdc in back ridge of second ch from hook *(Fig. 2, page 31)* and each ch across; slip st in next sc on Edging, finish off.

Repeat for second Tie in remaining marked sc.

FEATURES
Wing (Make 2)
With Blue, ch 12.

Rnd 1 (Right side)**:** Slip st in second ch from hook and in next ch, hdc in next ch, dc in next 2 chs, tr in next 3 chs, dc in next ch, hdc in next ch, 4 sc in last ch; working in free loops of beginning ch, hdc in next ch, dc in next ch, tr in next 3 chs, dc in next 2 chs, hdc in next ch, slip st in next 2 chs; join with slip st to first slip st, finish off.

Eye Patch (Make 2)
OUTER
With Tan, ch 4.

Rnd 1 (Right side)**:** 9 Dc in fourth ch from hook; join with slip st to first dc.

Note: Mark Rnd 1 as **right** side.

Rnd 2: Ch 2 (**does not count as a st**), 2 dc in same st as joining and in each dc around; join with slip st to first dc: 18 dc.

Rnd 3: Ch 1, sc in same st as joining, 2 sc in next dc, (sc in next dc, 2 sc in next dc) around; join with slip st to first sc: 27 sc.

Rnd 4: Ch 1, sc in same st as joining and in next sc, 2 sc in next sc, (sc in next 2 sc, 2 sc in next sc) around; join with slip st to first sc, finish off leaving a long end for sewing: 36 sc.

With a double strand of Orange, embroider a line around the edge of the Outer Eye Patch using running stitch *(see Embroidery Stitches, page 31)*.

INNER
With Blue, ch 2.

Rnd 1 (Right side)**:** 6 Sc in second ch from hook; join with slip st to first sc.

Note: Mark Rnd 1 as **right** side.

Rnd 2: Ch 1, 2 sc in same st as joining and in each sc around; join with slip st to first sc: 12 sc.

Rnd 3: Ch 1, sc in same st as joining, 2 sc in next sc, (sc in next sc, 2 sc in next sc) around; join with slip st to first sc: 18 sc.

Rnd 4: Ch 1, sc in same st as joining and in next sc, 2 sc in next sc, (sc in next 2 sc, 2 sc in next sc) around; join with slip st to first sc, finish off leaving a long end for sewing: 24 sc.

Sew **wrong** side of Inner Eye Patch to **right** side of Outer Eye Patch.

Eye (Make 2)
OUTER
With White, ch 2.

Rnd 1 (Right side)**:** 6 Sc in second ch from hook; join with slip st to first sc.

Note: Mark Rnd 1 as **right** side.

Rnd 2: Ch 1, 2 sc in same st as joining and in each sc around; join with slip st to first sc, finish off leaving a long end for sewing: 12 sc.

CENTER

With Black, ch 2.

Rnd 1 (Right side)**:** 4 Sc in second ch from hook; join with slip st to first sc, finish off leaving a long end for sewing.

Sew **wrong** side of Center to **right** side of Outer Eye.

FINISHING

Using photo as a guide for placement and with **right** side of all pieces facing:

Sew Outer Eye to Inner Eye Patch.

Sew Outer Eye Patch to head.

With Blue, sew Wings to Body.

With a double strand of Orange, embroider feet using straight stitch.

With a double strand of Orange, embroider beak using satin stitch.

HIPPO

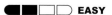 **EASY**

Finished Size: 7½" wide x 6¾" long (19 cm x 17 cm) excluding Ears

SHOPPING LIST

Yarn (Medium Weight) 🔵4
[1.75 ounces, 80 yards
(50 grams, 73 meters) per ball]:
☐ Yellow - 45 yards (41 meters)
☐ Blue - 35 yards (32 meters)
☐ Black - small amount

Crochet Hook
☐ Size G (4 mm)
or size needed for gauge

Additional Supplies
☐ Yarn needle

GAUGE INFORMATION
11 sc and 12.5 rows = 3" (7.5 cm)
Gauge Swatch: 3" wide x 2⅞" high
(7.5 cm x 7.25 cm)
With Blue, ch 12.
Row 1: Sc in second ch from hook
and in each ch across: 11 sc.
Rows 2-12: Ch 1, turn; sc in each sc
across.
Finish off.

STITCH GUIDE

SINGLE CROCHET 2 TOGETHER
(abbreviated sc2tog)
Pull up a loop in each of next 2 sts, YO
and draw through all 3 loops on hook
(counts as one sc).

HEAD
With Blue and beginning at top of
Head, ch 19.

Row 1 (Wrong side)**:** 2 Sc in second ch
from hook, sc in each ch across to last
ch, 2 sc in last ch: 20 sc.

Note: Loop a short piece of yarn
around the **back** of any stitch on
Row 1 to mark **right** side.

Rows 2 and 3: Ch 1, turn; 2 sc in first
sc, sc in each sc across to last sc, 2 sc
in last sc: 24 sc.

Rows 4-13: Ch 1, turn; sc in each sc
across.

Edging: Ch 1, turn; sc in each sc
across; sc evenly across end of
rows; working in free loops of
beginning ch (*Fig. 4, page 31*), sc
in ch at base of first sc and in next
ch, place marker in sc just made for
Tie placement, sc in each ch across
to last 2 chs, place marker in last sc
made for Tie placement, sc in last
2 chs; sc evenly across end of rows;
join with slip st to first sc, finish off.

Tie
With **right** side facing, join Yellow
with slip st in either marked sc on
Edging, remove marker; ch 52, hdc
in back ridge of second ch from
hook (*Fig. 2, page 31*) and each ch
across; slip st in next sc on Edging,
finish off.

Repeat for second Tie in remaining
marked sc.

MUZZLE

With Yellow and beginning at top of Muzzle, ch 21.

Row 1 (Wrong side)**:** 2 Sc in second ch from hook, sc in each ch across to last ch, 2 sc in last ch: 22 sc.

Note: Mark the **back** of Row 1 as **right** side.

Rows 2-4: Ch 1, turn; 2 sc in first sc, sc in each sc across to last sc, 2 sc in last sc: 28 sc.

Rows 5-13: Ch 1, turn; sc in each sc across.

Rows 14 and 15: Ch 1, turn; beginning in first sc, sc2tog, sc in each sc across to last 2 sc, sc2tog: 24 sc.

Edging: Ch 1, turn; beginning in first sc, sc2tog, sc in each sc across to last 2 sc, sc2tog; sc evenly across end of rows; working in free loops of beginning ch, sc in ch at base of first sc and in each ch across; sc evenly across end of rows; join with slip st to first sc, finish off.

With Blue, embroider a line around the edging using running stitch *(see Embroidery Stitches, page 31).*

FEATURES

Ear (Make 2)

With Blue, ch 6.

Rnd 1 (Right side)**:** Slip st in second ch from hook, sc in next ch, hdc in next ch, dc in next ch, 6 dc in last ch; working in free loops of beginning ch, dc in next ch, hdc in next ch, sc in next ch, slip st in next ch; finish off leaving a long end for sewing.

Eye (Make 2)

With Black, ch 2.

Rnd 1 (Right side)**:** 6 Sc in second ch from hook; join with slip st to first sc, finish off leaving a long end for sewing.

FINISHING

Using photo as a guide for placement and with **right** side of all pieces facing:
With Black, backstitch mouth and straight stitch nostrils on Muzzle.
Overlapping approximately 4 rows, sew top of Muzzle over bottom of Head.
Sew Ears to Head Edging.
Sew Eyes to Head.

ELEPHANT

 **EASY**

Finished Size: 7½" wide x 6½" long (19 cm x 16.5 cm) excluding Ears & Trunk

Shown on page 23.

SHOPPING LIST

Yarn (Medium Weight) 4

[1.75 ounces, 80 yards
(50 grams, 73 meters) per ball]:
- ☐ Grey - 85 yards (77.5 meters)
- ☐ White - 20 yards (18.5 meters)
- ☐ Black - small amount
- ☐ Pink - small amount

Crochet Hook
- ☐ Size G (4 mm)
  or size needed for gauge

Additional Supplies
- ☐ Yarn needle

GAUGE INFORMATION

11 sc and 12.5 rows = 3" (7.5 cm)
Gauge Swatch: 3" wide x 2⅞" high
  (7.5 cm x 7.25 cm)
With Grey, ch 12.
Row 1: Sc in second ch from hook
and in each ch across: 11 sc.
Rows 2-12: Ch 1, turn; sc in each sc
across.
Finish off.

STITCH GUIDE

SINGLE CROCHET 2 TOGETHER
  (abbreviated sc2tog)
Pull up a loop in each of next 2 sts, YO
and draw through all 3 loops on hook
(**counts as one sc**).

DOUBLE CROCHET 2 TOGETHER
  (abbreviated dc2tog)
(YO, insert hook in **next** sc, YO and
pull up a loop, YO and draw through
2 loops on hook) twice, YO and draw
through all 3 loops on hook (**counts
as one dc**).

HEAD

With Grey and beginning at top of
Head, ch 21.

Row 1 (Wrong side)**:** 2 Sc in second ch
from hook, sc in each ch across to last
ch, 2 sc in last ch: 22 sc.

Note: Loop a short piece of yarn
around the **back** of any stitch on
Row 1 to mark **right** side.

Rows 2 and 3: Ch 1, turn; 2 sc in first
sc, sc in each sc across to last sc, 2 sc
in last sc: 26 sc.

Rows 4-23: Ch 1, turn; sc in each sc
across.

Rows 24 and 25: Ch 1, turn;
beginning in first sc, sc2tog, sc in
each sc across to last 2 sc, sc2tog:
22 sc.

Edging: Ch 1, turn; beginning in
first sc, sc2tog, sc in each sc across
to last 2 sc, sc2tog; sc evenly across
end of rows; working in free loops
of beginning ch (*Fig. 4, page 31*), sc
in ch at base of first sc and in next
ch, place marker in sc just made for
Tie placement, sc in each ch across
to last 2 chs, place marker in last sc
made for Tie placement, sc in last
2 chs; sc evenly across end of rows;
join with slip st to first sc, finish off.

Tie

With **right** side facing, join White
with slip st in either marked sc on
Edging, remove marker; ch 52, hdc
in back ridge of second ch from
hook (*Fig. 2, page 31*) and each ch
across; slip st in next sc on Edging,
finish off.

Repeat for second Tie in remaining
marked sc.

FEATURES

Ears

LEFT

With Grey, ch 13.

Row 1 (Wrong side)**:** 2 Sc in second ch from hook, sc in each ch across to last ch, 2 sc in last ch: 14 sc.

Note: Mark the **back** of Row 1 as **right** side.

Rows 2 and 3: Ch 1, turn; 2 sc in first sc, sc in each sc across to last sc, 2 sc in last sc: 18 sc.

Rows 4-8: Ch 1, turn; sc in each sc across.

Row 9: Ch 1, turn; hdc in first sc, dc in next 6 sc, hdc in next sc, slip st in next 3 sc, hdc in next sc, dc in next 5 sc, hdc in last sc.

Edging: Ch 1, turn; hdc in first hdc, dc in next 7 sts, hdc in next slip st, slip st in next 3 sts, hdc in next dc, dc in next 4 dc, (dc, hdc) in last hdc; sc evenly across end of rows; working in free loops of beginning ch, sc in ch at base of first sc and in each ch across; sc evenly across end of rows; join with slip st to first hdc, finish off.

RIGHT

Work same as Left Ear through Row 8: 18 sc.

Row 9: Ch 1, turn; hdc in first sc, dc in next 5 sc, hdc in next sc, slip st in next 3 sc, hdc in next sc, dc in next 6 sc, hdc in last sc.

Edging: Ch 1, turn; (hdc, dc) in first hdc, dc in next 4 dc, hdc in next dc, slip st in next 3 sts, hdc in next slip st, dc in next 7 sts, hdc in last hdc; sc evenly across end of rows; working in free loops of beginning ch, sc in ch at base of first sc and in each ch across; sc evenly across end of rows; join with slip st to first hdc, finish off.

Trunk

With Grey, ch 4.

Row 1 (Right side)**:** 2 Sc in second ch from hook, sc in next ch, 2 sc in last ch: 5 sc.

Note: Mark Row 1 as **right** side.

Row 2: Ch 1, turn; 2 sc in first sc, sc in next 3 sc, 2 sc in last sc: 7 sc.

Rows 3-7: Ch 1, turn; sc in each sc across.

Row 8: Ch 1, turn; beginning in first sc, sc2tog, sc in next 3 sc, sc2tog: 5 sc.

Row 9: Ch 1, turn; 2 sc in first sc, sc in next 2 sc, sc2tog.

Row 10: Ch 1, turn; beginning in first sc, sc2tog, sc in next 2 sc, 2 sc in last sc.

Row 11: Ch 1, turn; 2 sc in first sc, sc in next 2 sc, sc2tog.

Row 12: Ch 1, turn; sc in each sc across.

Rows 13 and 14: Repeat Rows 10 and 11.

Row 15: Ch 1, turn; beginning in first st, sc2tog, sc in next 2 sc, 2 sc in last sc.

Row 16: Ch 1, turn; 2 sc in first sc, sc in next 2 sc, dc2tog.

Rows 17-20: Repeat Rows 15 and 16 twice.

Edging: Ch 1, turn; beginning in first st, sc2tog, sc in next 2 sc, 2 sc in last sc; sc evenly across end of rows; working in free loops of beginning ch, sc in each ch across; sc evenly across end of rows; join with slip st to first sc, finish off.

With White, embroider a line around the edging using running stitch *(see Embroidery Stitches, page 31)*.

Eye (Make 2)

With Black, ch 2.

Rnd 1 (Right side)**:** 6 Sc in second ch from hook; join with slip st to first sc, finish off leaving a long end for sewing.

FLOWER

With Pink, ch 4; join with slip st to form a ring.

Rnd 1 (Right side): Ch 1, 6 sc in ring; join with slip st to first sc, finish off leaving a long end for sewing.

Note: Mark Rnd 1 as **right** side.

Rnd 2: With **right** side facing, join White with slip st in same st as joining; ch 1, (3 dc, ch 1, slip st) in same st, (slip st, ch 1, 3 dc, ch 1, slip st) in each sc around; finish off.

FINISHING

Using photo as a guide for placement and with **right** side of all pieces facing:

With Grey, sew Ears to **right** side of Head Edging.

With Grey, sew Trunk to Head.

Sew Eyes to Head.

Sew Flower to corner of Ear.

BUTTERFLY

 **EASY**

Finished Size: 9" wide x 7" long (23 cm x 18 cm)

SHOPPING LIST

Yarn (Medium Weight)

[1.75 ounces, 80 yards
(50 grams, 73 meters) per ball]:

☐ Purple - 50 yards (45.5 meters)

☐ Blue - 35 yards (32 meters)

☐ Pink - 20 yards (18.5 meters)

☐ White - small amount

☐ Black - small amount

Crochet Hook

☐ Size G (4 mm)

or size needed for gauge

Additional Supplies

☐ Yarn needle

GAUGE INFORMATION

11 sc and 12.5 rows = 3" (7.5 cm)

Gauge Swatch: 3" wide x 2⅞" high
(7.5 cm x 7.25 cm)

With Blue, ch 12.

Row 1: Sc in second ch from hook
and in each ch across: 11 sc.

Rows 2-12: Ch 1, turn; sc in each sc
across.

Finish off.

STITCH GUIDE

SINGLE CROCHET 2 TOGETHER
 (abbreviated sc2tog)
Pull up a loop in each of next 2 sts, YO
and draw through all 3 loops on hook
(counts as one sc).

BODY

With Blue and beginning at top of
Head, ch 5.

Row 1 (Wrong side)**:** 2 Sc in second
ch from hook, sc in next 2 chs, 2 sc in
last ch: 6 sc.

Note: Loop a short piece of yarn
around the **back** of any stitch on
Row 1 to mark **right** side.

Rows 2 and 3: Ch 1, turn; 2 sc in first
sc, sc in each sc across to last sc, 2 sc
in last sc: 10 sc.

Rows 4-6: Ch 1, turn; sc in each sc
across.

Rows 7-9: Ch 1, turn; beginning in
first sc, sc2tog, sc in each sc across to
last 2 sc, sc2tog: 4 sc.

Row 10: Ch 1, turn; sc in each sc
across.

Rows 11-13: Ch 1, turn; 2 sc in first
sc, sc in each sc across to last sc, 2 sc
in last sc: 10 sc.

Rows 14-18: Ch 1, turn; sc in each sc
across.

Row 19 (Decrease row)**:** Ch 1, turn;
beginning in first sc, sc2tog, sc in
each sc across to last 2 sc, sc2tog:
8 sc.

Row 20: Ch 1, turn; sc in each sc
across.

Rows 21-24: Repeat Rows 19 and
20 twice: 4 sc.

Row 25: Ch 1, turn; beginning in first
sc, sc2tog twice: 2 sc.

Row 26: Ch 1, turn; beginning in first
sc, sc2tog: one sc.

Edging: Ch 1, do **not** turn; sc evenly
across end of rows, place marker in
last sc made for Antenna placement;

working in free loops of beginning ch *(Fig. 4, page 31)*, sc in ch at base of first sc and in each ch across; sc in first row, place marker in sc just made for Antenna placement, sc evenly across end of remaining rows; (sc, ch 1, sc) in remaining st on Row 26; join with slip st to first sc, finish off.

Antenna: With **right** side facing, join Pink with slip st in first marked sc, remove marker, ch 4; finish off leaving a ½" (12 mm) end.

Repeat for second Antenna.

OUTER WINGS
Right
With Purple, ch 16.

Row 1 (Right side)**:** 2 Sc in second ch from hook, sc in each ch across to last ch, 2 sc in last ch: 17 sc.

Note: Mark Row 1 as **right** side.

Row 2: Ch 1, turn; 2 sc in first sc, sc in each sc across to last sc, 2 sc in last sc: 19 sc.

Row 3: Ch 1, turn; 2 sc in first sc, sc in next 8 sc, dc in next 9 sc, 2 dc in last sc: 21 sts.

Row 4: Ch 2 (**does not count as a st, now and throughout**), turn; 2 dc in first dc, dc in next 10 dc, sc in last 10 sc: 22 sts.

Row 5: Ch 2, turn; dc in first sc and in each st across to last dc, 2 dc in last dc: 23 dc.

Row 6: Ch 2, turn; 2 dc in first dc, dc in next 12 dc, sc in last 10 dc: 24 sts.

Row 7: Ch 1, turn; sc in first 10 sc, dc in last 14 dc.

Row 8: Ch 2, turn; dc in first 14 dc, sc in last 10 sc.

Row 9: Ch 1, turn; beginning in first sc, sc2tog, place marker in sc just made for st placement, dc in next 6 sc, sc in next sc, slip st in next sc, sc2tog, dc in next 10 dc, sc2tog; sc evenly across end of rows; working in free loops of beginning ch, sc in first ch, place marker in sc just made for Outer Wing assembly, sc in next 14 chs, place marker in last sc made for Outer Wing assembly; sc evenly across end of rows.

Row 10: Do **not** turn; beginning in marked sc, sc2tog, remove marker, dc in next 5 dc, sc in next sc, slip st in next slip st, sc in next 12 sts, slip st in next st, leave remaining sts unworked; finish off.

Left
Work same as Right Wing, page 25, through Row 2: 19 sc.

Row 3: Ch 2, turn; 2 dc in first sc, dc in next 9 sc, sc in next 8 sc, 2 sc in last sc: 21 sts.

Row 4: Ch 1, turn; sc in first 10 sc, dc in next 10 dc, 2 dc in last dc: 22 sts.

Row 5: Ch 2, turn; 2 dc in first dc, dc in next dc and in each st across: 23 dc.

Row 6: Ch 1, turn; sc in first 10 dc, dc in next 12 dc, 2 dc in last dc: 24 sts.

Row 7: Ch 2, turn; dc in first 14 dc, sc in last 10 sc.

Row 8: Ch 1, turn; sc in first 10 sc, dc in last 14 dc.

Row 9: Ch 1, turn; beginning in first dc, sc2tog, place marker in sc just made for st placement, dc in next 10 dc, sc2tog, slip st in next sc, sc in next sc, dc in next 6 sc, sc2tog; sc evenly across end of rows; working in free loops of beginning ch, sc in first ch, place marker in sc just made for Outer Wing assembly, sc in next 14 chs, place marker in last sc made for Outer Wing assembly; sc evenly across end of rows.

Row 10: Do **not** turn; sc in marked sc and in next 11 sts, remove marker, slip st in next slip st, sc in next sc, dc in next 5 dc, sc2tog, slip st in next st, leave remaining sts unworked; finish off.

With **wrong** sides of Right and Left Wing together and matching marked sts, whipstitch pieces together with Purple *(Fig. A)*, working through **both** loops on **both** pieces and beginning and ending in marked sts; remove markers.

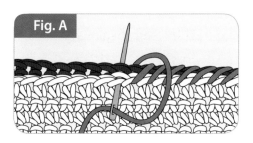

Fig. A

INNER WINGS
Right
With Pink, ch 10.

Row 1 (Right side)**:** 2 Sc in second ch from hook, sc in each ch across to last ch, 2 sc in last ch: 11 sc.

Note: Mark Row 1 as **right** side.

Row 2: Ch 1, turn; 2 sc in first sc, sc in next 9 sc, 2 dc in last sc: 13 sts.

Row 3: Ch 1, turn; 2 sc in first dc, sc in next 4 sts, dc in next 7 sc, 2 dc in last sc: 15 sts.

Row 4: Ch 2, turn; 2 dc in first dc, dc in next 8 dc, sc in last 6 sc: 16 sts.

Row 5: Ch 1, turn; sc in first 6 sc, dc in last 10 dc.

Row 6: Ch 1, turn; beginning in first dc, sc2tog, sc in next 6 dc, sc2tog, slip st in next sc, dc in next 3 sc, sc2tog: 13 sts.

Edging: Ch 1, turn; beginning in first sc, sc2tog, sc in next 2 dc, slip st in next 2 sts, sc in next sc, dc in next 4 sc, sc2tog; sc evenly across end of rows; working in free loops of beginning ch, sc in first ch, place marker in last sc made for Inner Wing assembly, sc in next 9 chs, place marker in last sc made for Inner Wing assembly; sc evenly across end of rows; join with slip st to first sc, finish off.

Left

Work same as Right Inner Wing through Row 2: 13 sts.

Row 3: Ch 2, turn; 2 dc in first dc, dc in next 7 sts, sc in next 4 sc, 2 sc in last sc: 15 sts.

Row 4: Ch 1, turn; sc in first 6 sc, dc in next 8 dc, 2 dc in last dc: 16 sts.

Row 5: Ch 2, turn; dc in first 10 dc, sc in last 6 sc.

Row 6: Ch 1, turn; beginning in first sc, sc2tog, dc in next 3 sc, slip st in next sc, sc2tog, sc in next 6 dc, sc2tog: 13 sts.

Edging: Ch 1, turn; beginning in first sc, sc2tog, dc in next 4 sc, sc in next sc, slip st in next 2 sts, sc in next 2 dc, sc2tog; sc evenly across end of rows; working in free loops of beginning ch, sc in first ch, place marker in last sc made for Inner Wing assembly, sc in next 9 chs, place marker in last sc made for Inner Wing assembly; sc evenly across end of rows; join with slip st to first sc, finish off.

Thread yarn needle with Pink. With **wrong** sides of Right and Left Wing together and matching marked sts, whipstitch pieces together, working through **both** loops on **both** pieces and beginning and ending in marked sts; remove markers.

TIE (Make 2)

With Blue, ch 52.
Hdc in back ridge of second ch from hook *(Fig. 2, page 31)* and each ch across; finish off leaving a long end for sewing

EYE (Make 2)

With Black, ch 2.

Rnd 1 (Right side)**:** (Sc, slip st) in second ch from hook; finish off leaving a long end for sewing.

FINISHING

Using photo as a guide for placement, page 25, and with **right** side of all pieces facing:
Place Inner Wings and Outer Wings together. With White and working through both layers, embroider a line around the edge of Inner Wings using running stitch *(see Embroidery Stitches, page 31)*.
With a double strand of White, add mouth using backstitch.
Sew Eyes to head.
With Blue, sew Body to Inner Wings.
Sew Ties to Outer Wings.

FOX

 **EASY**

Finished Size: 7½" wide x 8" long (19 cm x 20.5 cm)

SHOPPING LIST

Yarn (Medium Weight)

[1.75 ounces, 80 yards
(50 grams, 73 meters) per ball]:

☐ Red - 40 yards (36.5 meters)

☐ Off White - 25 yards (23 meters)

☐ Black - 15 yards (13.5 meters)

Crochet Hook

☐ Size G (4 mm)

or size needed for gauge

Additional Supplies

☐ Yarn needle

GAUGE INFORMATION

11 sc and 12.5 rows = 3" (7.5 cm)

Gauge Swatch: 3" wide x 2⅞" high
(7.5 cm x 7.25 cm)

With Red, ch 12.

Row 1: Sc in second ch from hook
and in each ch across: 11 sc.

Rows 2-12: Ch 1, turn; sc in each sc
across.

Finish off.

STITCH GUIDE

SINGLE CROCHET 2 TOGETHER
(abbreviated sc2tog)
Pull up a loop in each of next 2 sc, YO
and draw through all 3 loops on hook
(counts as one sc).

HEAD

With Red and beginning at top of
Head, ch 26.

Row 1 (Right side)**:** Sc in second ch
from hook and in each ch across: 25 sc.

Note: Loop a short piece of yarn
around any stitch to mark Row 1 as
right side.

Rows 2-13: Ch 1, turn; sc in each sc
across.

Row 14: Ch 1, turn; sc in each sc across
changing to Black in last sc *(Fig. 3a,
page 31)*; cut Red.

Row 15: Ch 1, turn; sc in first sc, skip
next sc, sc in next 10 sc, 3 sc in next
sc, sc in next 10 sc, skip next sc, sc
in last sc.

Row 16: Ch 1, turn; sc in first sc, skip
next sc, sc in next 10 sc, 3 sc in next sc,
sc in next 10 sc, skip next sc, sc in last
sc changing to Off White; cut Black.

Rows 17-24: Ch 1, turn; sc in first sc,
skip next sc, sc in next 10 sc, 3 sc in
next sc, sc in next 10 sc, skip next sc,
sc in last sc.

Edging: Ch 1, turn; sc in first sc, skip
next sc, sc in next 10 sc, 3 sc in next
sc, sc in next 10 sc, skip next sc, sc in
last sc; sc evenly across end of rows;
working in free loops of beginning
ch *(Fig. 4, page 31)*, sc in first 4 chs,
place marker in last sc made for
Tie placement, sc in next 17 chs,
place marker in last sc made for Tie
placement, sc in next 4 chs; sc evenly
across end of rows; join with slip st to
first sc, finish off.

Tie

With **right** side facing, join Red with
slip st in either marked sc on Edging,
remove marker; ch 52, hdc in back
ridge of second ch from hook *(Fig. 2,
page 31)* and each ch across; slip st in
next sc on Edging, finish off.

Repeat for second Tie in remaining
marked sc.

Eye (Make 2)

OUTER

With Off White, ch 2.

Rnd 1 (Right side)**:** 7 Sc in second ch from hook; join with slip st to first sc.

Note: Mark Rnd 1 as **right** side.

Rnd 2: Ch 1, 2 sc in same st as joining and in each sc around; join with slip st to first sc, finish off leaving a long end for sewing.

CENTER

With Black, ch 2.

Rnd 1 (Right side)**:** 6 Sc in second ch from hook; join with slip st to first sc, finish off leaving a long end for sewing.

Sew **wrong** side of Center to **right** side of Outer Eye; then add eyelashes using straight stitches *(see Embroidery Stitches, page 31).*

FINISHING

Using photo as a guide for placement and with **right** side of all pieces facing:

Sew Ears and Eyes to Head.

Using a double strand of Black, add a backstitch mouth and a satin stitch nose.

FEATURES

Ear (Make 2)

With Black, ch 2.

Row 1 (Right side)**:** 2 Sc in second ch from hook.

Note: Mark Row 1 as **right** side.

Row 2: Ch 1, turn; 2 sc in each sc across: 4 sc.

Row 3: Ch 1, turn; 2 sc in first sc, sc in next 2 sc, 2 sc in last sc: 6 sc.

Rows 4-6: Ch 1, turn; sc in each sc across.

Row 7: Ch 1, turn; beginning in first sc, sc2tog, sc in next 2 sc, sc2tog; finish off leaving a long end for sewing: 4 sc.

GENERAL INSTRUCTIONS

ABBREVIATIONS

ch(s)	chain(s)
cm	centimeters
dc	double crochet(s)
dc2tog	double crochet 2 together
hdc	half double crochet(s)
mm	millimeters
Rnd(s)	Round(s)
sc	single crochet(s)
sc2tog	single crochet 2 together
st(s)	stitch(es)
tr	treble crochet(s)
YO	yarn over

SYMBOLS & TERMS

( ) or [ ] — work enclosed instructions **as many** times as specified by the number immediately following **or** work all enclosed instructions in the stitch or space indicated **or** contains explanatory remarks.

colon (:) — the number(s) after a colon at the end of a row or round denote(s) the number of stitches you should have on that row or round.

GAUGE

Exact gauge is essential for proper size. Before beginning your Bib, make the sample swatch given in the individual instructions in the yarn and hook specified. After completing the swatch, measure it, counting your stitches and rows carefully. If your swatch is larger or smaller than specified, make another, changing hook size to get the correct gauge. Keep trying until you find the size hook that will give you the specified gauge.

MARKERS

Markers are used to help distinguish the beginning of each round being worked. Place a 2" (5 cm) scrap piece of yarn before the first stitch of each round, moving marker after each round is complete.

Yarn Weight Symbol & Names	LACE 0	SUPER FINE 1	FINE 2	LIGHT 3	MEDIUM 4	BULKY 5	SUPER BULKY 6	JUMBO 7
Type of Yarns in Category	Fingering, size 10 crochet thread	Sock, Fingering, Baby	Sport, Baby	DK, Light Worsted	Worsted, Afghan, Aran	Chunky, Craft, Rug	Super Bulky, Roving	Jumbo, Roving
Crochet Gauge* Ranges in Single Crochet to 4" (10 cm)	32-42 sts**	21-32 sts	16-20 sts	12-17 sts	11-14 sts	8-11 sts	6-9 sts	5 sts and fewer
Advised Hook Size Range	Steel*** 6 to 8, Regular hook B-1	B-1 to E-4	E-4 to 7	7 to I-9	I-9 to K-10½	K-10½ to M/N-13	M/N-13 to Q	Q and larger

*GUIDELINES ONLY: The chart above reflects the most commonly used gauges and hook sizes for specific yarn categories.

** Lace weight yarns are usually crocheted with larger hooks to create lacy openwork patterns. Accordingly, a gauge range is difficult to determine. Always follow the gauge stated in your pattern.

*** Steel crochet hooks are sized differently from regular hooks–the higher the number, the smaller the hook, which is the reverse of regular hook sizing.

CROCHET TERMINOLOGY	
UNITED STATES	INTERNATIONAL
slip stitch (slip st) =	single crochet (sc)
single crochet (sc) =	double crochet (dc)
half double crochet (hdc) =	half treble crochet (htr)
double crochet (dc) =	treble crochet (tr)
treble crochet (tr) =	double treble crochet (dtr)
double treble crochet (dtr) =	triple treble crochet (ttr)
triple treble crochet (tr tr) =	quadruple treble crochet (qtr)
skip =	miss

■□□□ BEGINNER	Projects for first-time crocheters using basic stitches. Minimal shaping.
■■□□ EASY	Projects using yarn with basic stitches, repetitive stitch patterns, simple color changes, and simple shaping and finishing.
■■■□ INTERMEDIATE	Projects using a variety of techniques, such as basic lace patterns or color patterns, mid-level shaping and finishing.
■■■■ EXPERIENCED	Projects with intricate stitch patterns, techniques and dimension, such as non-repeating patterns, multi-color techniques, fine threads, small hooks, detailed shaping and refined finishing.

JOINING WITH SC

When instructed to join with a sc, begin with a slip knot on the hook. Insert hook in stitch or space indicated, YO and pull up a loop, YO and draw through both loops on hook.

BACK LOOPS ONLY

Work only in loop(s) indicated by arrow *(Fig. 1)*.

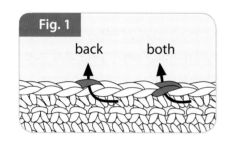

Fig. 1

back   both

BACK RIDGE OF A CHAIN

Work only in loops indicated by arrows *(Fig. 2)*.

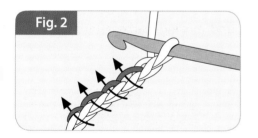

Fig. 2

CHANGING COLORS

Work the last stitch to within one step of completion, hook new yarn *(Fig. 3a or 3b)* and draw through both loops on hook. Cut old color and work over both ends.

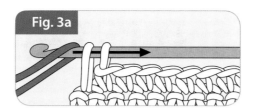

Fig. 3a

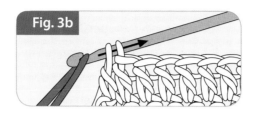

Fig. 3b

FREE LOOPS OF A CHAIN

When instructed to work in free loops of a chain, work in loop indicated by arrow *(Fig. 4)*.

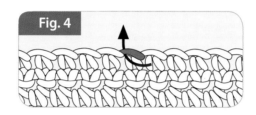

Fig. 4

EMBROIDERY STITCHES
Backstitch

The backstitch is worked from **right** to **left**. Come up at 1, go down at 2 and come up at 3 *(Fig. 5)*. The second stitch is made by going down at 1 and coming up at 4.

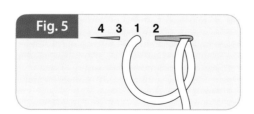

Fig. 5   4 3 1 2

Straight Stitch

Straight stitch is just what the name implies, a single, straight stitch. Come up at 1 and go down at 2 *(Fig. 6)*.

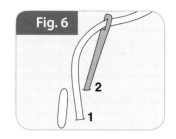

Fig. 6

Satin Stitch

Satin stitch is a series of straight stitches worked side-by-side so they touch but do not overlap *(Fig. 7a)* or come out of and go into the same stitch *(Fig. 7b)*. Come up at odd numbers and go down at even numbers.

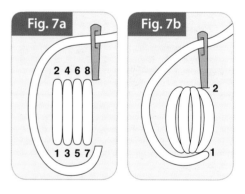

Fig. 7a   2 4 6 8   1 3 5 7

Fig. 7b

Running Stitch

Running stitch is a series of straight stitches that weave in and out of the fabric. Come up at 1, go down at 2, come up at 3, and go down at 4 *(Fig. 8)*. Continue in the same manner.

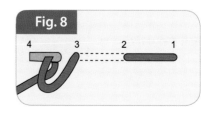

Fig. 8   4   3   2   1

YARN INFORMATION

The Bibs in this book were made using *Bernat® Handicrafter®* cotton yarn. Any brand of Medium Weight yarn may be used. It is best to refer to the yardage/meters when determining how many balls or skeins to purchase. Remember, to arrive at the finished size, it is the GAUGE/TENSION that is important, not the brand of yarn.

For your convenience, listed below are the specific colors used to create our photography models. Because yarn manufacturers make frequent changes in their product lines, you may sometimes find it necessary to use a substitute yarn or to search for the discontinued product at alternate suppliers (locally or online).

TIGER
Orange - #01628 Hot Orange
Black - #01040 Black Licorice
White - #01001 White

ZEBRA
Black - #01040 Black Licorice
White - #01001 White
Green - #01712 Hot Green

COW
White - #01001 White
Pink - #01740 Hot Pink
Black - #01040 Black Licorice
Purple - #01317 Hot Purple

GIRAFFE
Yellow - #01030 Pale Yellow
Tan - #01085 Jute
Brown - #01130 Warm Brown

OWL
Green - #01712 Hot Green
Blue - #01111 Mod Blue
Tan - #01085 Jute
Orange - #01699 Tangerine
White - #01001 White
Black - #01040 Black Licorice

HIPPO
Yellow - #01030 Pale Yellow
Blue - #01725 Blueberry
Black - #01040 Black Licorice

ELEPHANT
Grey - #01042 Overcast
White - #01001 White
Black - #01040 Black Licorice
Pink - #01740 Hot Pink

BUTTERFLY
Purple - #01318 Black Currant
Blue - #01742 Hot Blue
Pink - #01740 Hot Pink
White - #01001 White
Black - #01040 Black Licorice

FOX
Red - #01530 Country Red
Off White - #01002 Off White
Black - #01040 Black Licorice

CROCHET HOOKS																
U.S.	B-1	C-2	D-3	E-4	F-5	G-6	7	H-8	I-9	J-10	K-10½	L-11	M/N-13	N/P-15	P/Q	Q	S
Metric - mm	2.25	2.75	3.25	3.5	3.75	4	4.5	5	5.5	6	6.5	8	9	10	15	16	19

We have made every effort to ensure that these instructions are accurate and complete. We cannot, however, be responsible for human error, typographical mistakes, or variations in individual work.

Production Team: Instructional/Technical Editor - Linda A. Daley; Editorial Writer - Susan Frantz Wiles; Senior Graphic Artist - Lora Puls; Graphic Artist - Cailen Cochran; Photo Stylist - Lori Wenger; and Photographer - Jason Masters.